BOOK · 3

Photographs by
MIKE DAVIS

CONTENTS

Published by IPC Magazines Ltd., Fleetway House, Farringdon Street, London, England. Sole Agents for Australia and New Zealand: Gordon and Gotch Ltd.; South Africa: Central News Agency Ltd.; Rhodesia, Zambia and Malawi: Kingstons Ltd. Printing and binding by Istituto Italiana d'Arti Grafiche – Bergamo.
© IPC Magazines Ltd. 1970.

Magic Moments

John Gilpin and Gillian Shane showing tremendous joie de vivre during a rehearsal of Graduation Ball.

The **PRINCE**

THIS ballet was first produced at the Royal Opera House, Covent Garden, in 1957. It proved a tremendous success, not only for its choreographer, John Cranko, who was also responsible for the story, but for the composer of its music, Benjamin Britten, whose first ballet score this was.

It was an ambitious project and one that has taxed the resources of every theatre that has performed the ballet since 1957. In fact, not until early last year, when the ballet master of the Vienna State Opera, Wazlaw Orlikowsky, produced his version in Vienna were ballet lovers able to see *The Prince of the Pagodas* for the marvellous spectacle it was meant to be. It turned out to be wildly exciting and exhilarating to watch.

The story opens at the Court of the Middle Kingdom with the Compassionate Fool preparing for the arrival of the suitors of the Emperor's eldest daughter, Belle Epine. As the Court fills with nobles, heralds announce the arrival of the four Kings—the Kings of the North, South, East and West. With a flourish of trumpets, the Kings enter with their entourages.

(Continued on page 8)

Above: *The Compassionate Fool playfully dances with Belle Rose, the Emperor's younger daughter (Susie Kirnbauer).*

Below: *The four suitors at the Court of the Middle Kingdom compete for the hand of the Emperor's elder daughter who is heiress to the crown of the Middle Kingdom. Such a marriage would make the lucky one all-powerful.*

OF THE **P**AGODAS

Above: *The conceited and wicked Princess Belle Epine (Chrystl Zimmerl) refuses the union her father offers her and scorns the Kings.*
Right: *The King of the East, danced by leading male dancer, Paul Vondrak.* **Below:** *Two further scenes from this lavish production.*

In the meantime, the Emperor's younger daughter, Belle Rose, is in her boudoir dreaming of a handsome young prince who needs her love. She is awakened from her dreams by the Court Fool, who takes her to meet the four Kings, much to the annoyance of her jealous elder sister.

Suddenly, four huge frogs enter, bearing a golden casket for Belle Rose. On opening it she discovers a single rose, sent to her by the Prince of her dreams.

She asks the frogs to take her to the Prince and she is whisked away in a golden net to the land of the Pagodas. Alas, all she finds after further adventures is a great Salamander. However, he eventually turns out to be—yes, you've guessed it!—her Prince!

Together they return to her father's Court in the Middle Kingdom, only to find that he has been imprisoned in a cage by his ungrateful and wicked elder daughter, who has usurped his throne.

Fortunately, with the aid of the fairy Prince, and a little magic on the side, things are soon righted. They all live happily ever after—at least, all the Good Characters do!

Right: *In the land of the Pagodas.*

Right centre: *Princess Belle Rose finds herself being borne aloft as if in a dream.*

Far right: *Another change of scenery in this most lavish of ballets, which sometimes has as many as eighty dancers on-stage at the same time.*

Top left and top right: *The young princess, Belle Rose,*
performing a solo dance and a pas de deux with the Salamander,
who later turns out to be the Prince of her dreams.

Right: *The Salamander reaches up to grasp the hand of his love, Belle Rose.* **Below:** *The King of the North (Ludwig Musil) in a warlike dance by which he hopes to attract the attention of Belle Épine, the heiress to the Kingdom.*

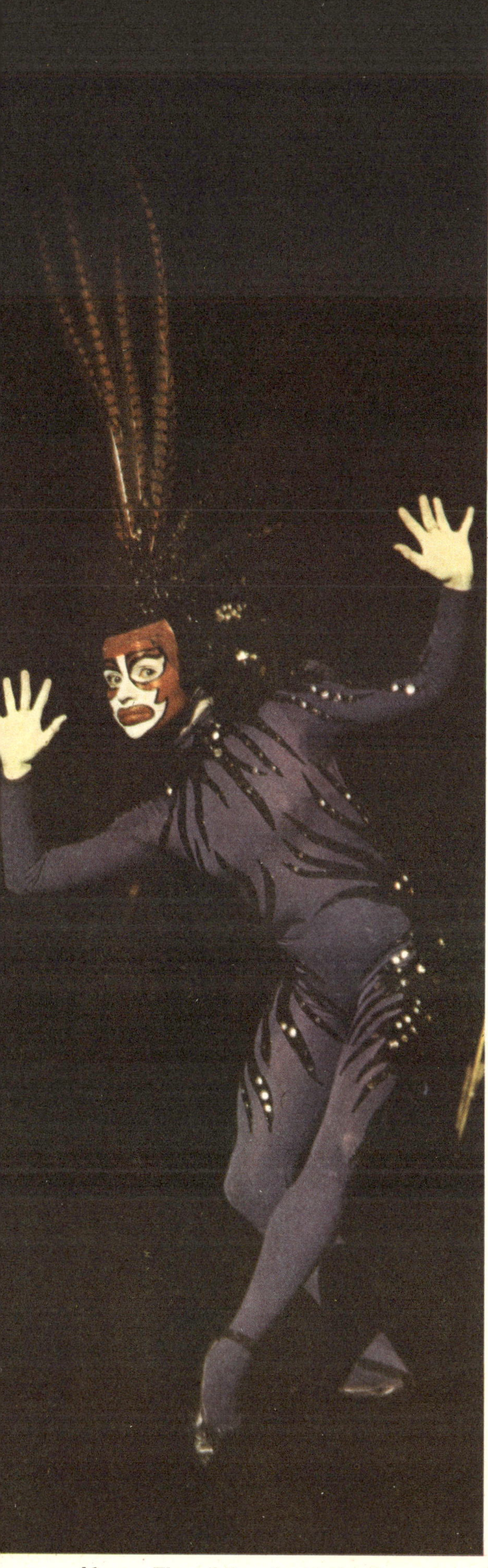

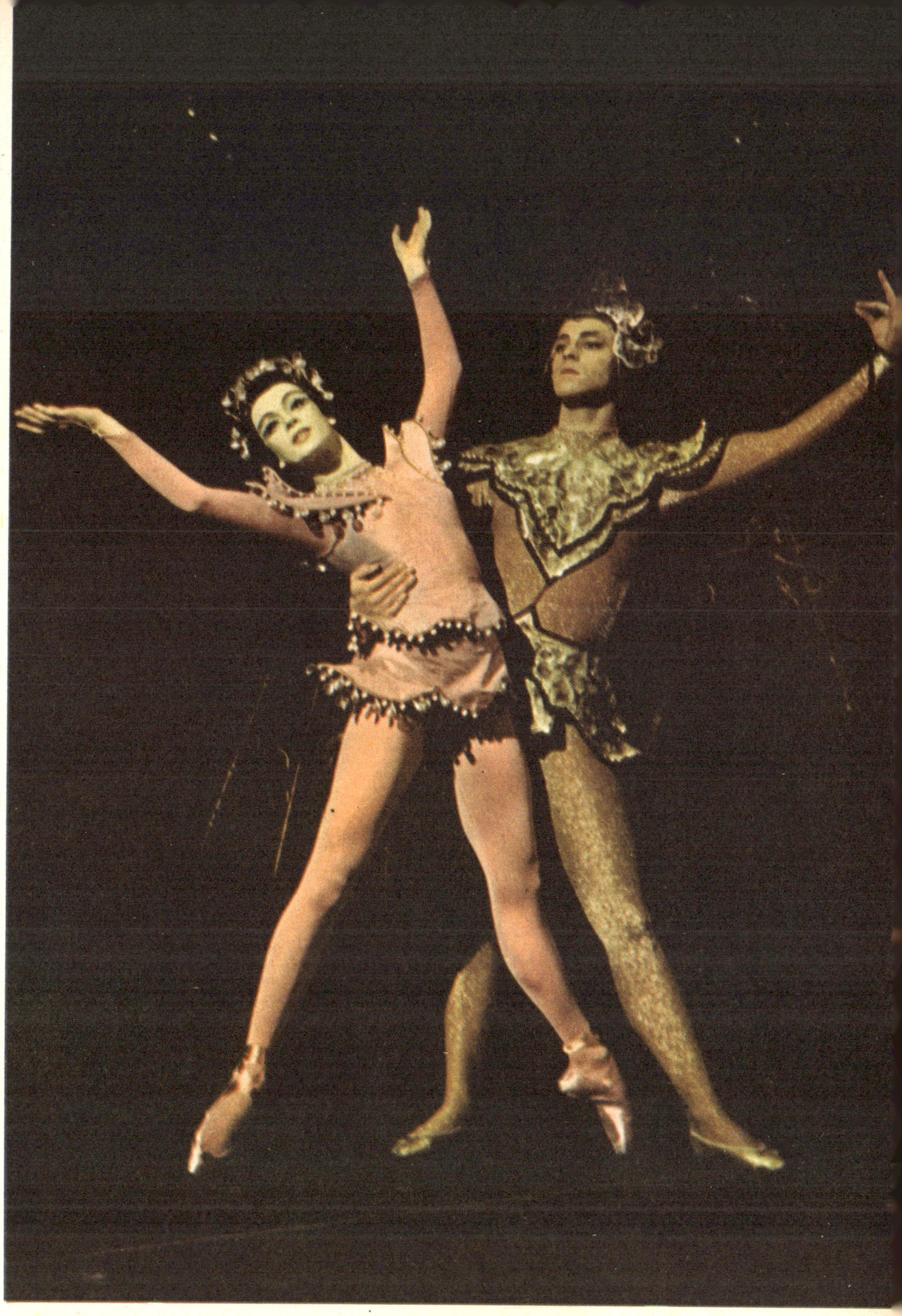

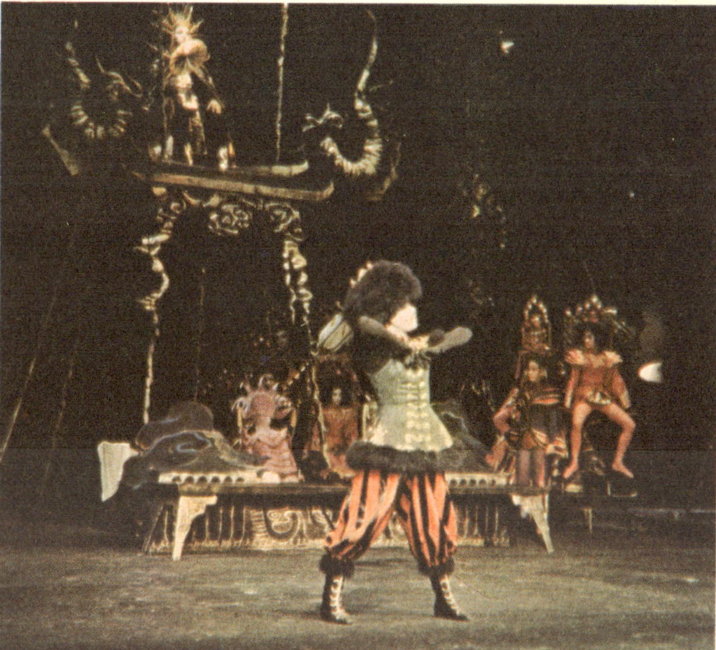

Above: *The evil Dwarf, wicked genius of the ballet and creature of the inhuman elder daughter of the Emperor.* **Above right:** *Another movement in the Prince's pas de deux with his beloved Belle Rose.*

Left: *Another scene from this lavish ballet which scintillates with weird and wonderful décor. Its huge sets need 60 scene-shifters to change them.*

Margaret Barbieri

IT IS not often that a young girl from the Corps de Ballet is called upon at a moment's notice to fill the star role in a major production. It is even rarer when this happens at London's Royal Opera House in Covent Garden.

When the performance is *Giselle*, possibly the most difficult title-role to fill in the whole ballet repertoire, it is even more amazing that a relatively inexperienced young dancer should be praised by critics and public alike. So tremendous was the audience's enthusiasm that the performance was literally stopped several times by applause. Margaret Barbieri had arrived!

It has been said that the title-role of *Giselle* demands such remarkable dramatic and technical qualities in a dancer that no ballerina under the age of 40 can adequately perform the part! Not only did this 21-year-old girl dance Giselle far more than adequately—she completely captured the hearts of all who saw her.

The story of *Giselle* is a simple but moving one. It is about an innocent village girl who falls in love with a handsome young stranger, named Albrecht, whom she meets in the forest.

Albrecht returns her love, but, unfortunately for Giselle, he is a nobleman in disguise and is already betrothed to someone else.

When poor Giselle learns the awful truth, she snatches Albrecht's sword and kills herself.

Albrecht, broken-hearted for the wrong he has done, visits Giselle's grave deep in the forest and is captured by a band of Wilis—young girls whose spirits haunt the forest glades!

The Wilis order Albrecht to dance until he dies, but he is saved by Giselle, who comes back from the grave and takes his place.

Left and far left: *Galina Samtsova and Andre Prokovsky in some of the dramatic movements which so admirably suit their Russian training. Their classical perfection often leaves an audience breathless.*

COMMAND PERFORMANCE

Above and left: *More shots of these superb artists in Jack Carter's The Unknown Island.*

Last year London's Festival Ballet celebrated its twentieth anniversary by holding a Royal Gala Performance in honour of Princess Margaret, Countess of Snowdon.

A FIRST NIGHT is always something special, but when Royalty is present it becomes an occasion.

It was certainly a wonderful occasion when the dancers of London's Festival Ballet Company performed before Princess Margaret at the London Coliseum, an historic theatre where the great Diaghilev staged many of his triumphs. The cast knew that the Princess is herself a balletomane, and a very knowledgeable one at that. As the President of the Royal Ballet, she takes a very active interest in its work, regularly attends performances, and, indeed, often goes to the dress rehearsals of new ballets.

To mark this occasion Festival Ballet presented an entirely new work, *The Unknown Island,* with Galina Samtsova and André Prokovsky dancing the leading roles. Jack Carter was the choreographer and the music was Berlioz's *Les Nuits d'Été,* a song-cycle of poems by Theophile Gautier. It was a fitting choice, as 1969 was the centenary of Berlioz's death.

There were also some Divertissements in the programme, including a pas classique danced by Wilfride Piollet and Cyril Atanassoff, who had been specially brought over from the Paris Opera.

Traditional classical ballet has always been a feature of Festival Ballet's programmes. This gala occasion was no exception.

Scheherazade

THIS one-act ballet can almost be called the trendsetter for the early part of this century, at least for scenery and costume, as when it was first produced by the great Diaghilev at the Paris Opéra in 1910, it caused a major sensation.

As soon as the curtain went up, the audience gasped in amazement and admiration at the vivid and glowing colours of the decor and the exotic costumes. The impact was such on many artists that the whole future of scenic design was influenced by this historic ballet.

The enormous success of *Scheherazade* was by no means due to the stunning decor alone. The great Nijinsky excelled himself in it, finding the ballet a perfect vehicle for his talents and style of dancing.

When Dr. Julian Braunsweg was Director General of the Festival Ballet, he revived this exciting and fantastic work, but, although it proved very popular, it was never quite the same without the original Bakst decor and the supreme magic of Nijinsky, despite the fact that Dr. Braunsweg had worked with Diaghilev on the original production.

The setting of the ballet is rather an ambiguous one. Though it has a strong Persian theme, the palace in which the action takes place is that of a mythical King Shahryar who, according to the story, appears to be the King of India and China. Judging by the size of his entourage, it would seem to be quite possible!

The curtain rises on the harem of the palace, where the King is relaxing with his wives on a huge divan. He looks worried at the news that his brother the Shah Zeman, has brought him, and ignores the dancing girls who seek to please him.

Suddenly, he decides to forget his worries and

go hunting. Zobeide, his chief wife, pleads to accompany him, but he angrily refuses her entreaties and leaves.

Shah Zeman is deeply jealous of the influence that Zobeide has over his brother, the King, and is busy plotting to undermine her position by making him doubt her loyalty and love. He tells him about a certain slave who has gained her affections.

Although the King is furious at the startling allegations that his brother has made about his wife, he agrees to return unexpectedly and surprise her.

He returns and finds Zobeide in the arms of the slave. Maddened with rage, he draws his scimitar and kills the slave. The wretched Zobeide, overwhelmed with despair, kills herself.

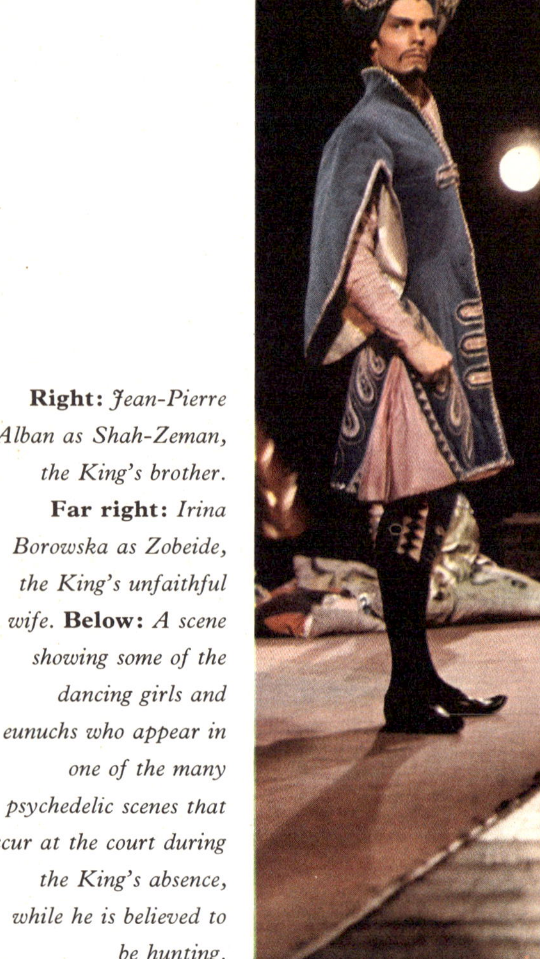

Right: *Jean-Pierre Alban as Shah-Zeman, the King's brother.* **Far right:** *Irina Borowska as Zobeide, the King's unfaithful wife.* **Below:** *A scene showing some of the dancing girls and eunuchs who appear in one of the many psychedelic scenes that occur at the court during the King's absence, while he is believed to be hunting.*

Peter White as Shahryar, surrounded by his various wives and dancing girls in his harem at the court in the opening scene of the ballet. It was the scintillating splendour of this scene which caused the furore at the Paris Opéra when Diaghilev presented this ballet, considered by some to be his most successful. The designer, Bakst, employed all the vivid and glowing colours he could, and this, combined with magnificent stage jewellery and clever lighting, made an unforgettable effect.

TOP STUDENTS

Danilova

FORMERLY Prima Ballerina of the Ballet Russe de Monte Carlo, and one of the truly great dancers of the world of ballet, Danilova is now teaching with the American Ballet Theater and at the Harkness Ballet Workshop in New York.

She was trained at the Imperial Maryinsky School in Leningrad, or St. Petersburg, as it was then known.

She is shown here in the costume of the Dying Swan, a role made famous by her great contemporary, Anna Pavlova.

DANCERS FROM OTHER LANDS

In the past decade the West has become increasingly aware of the dancing and culture of other, more exotic places.

Dancing is as old as Man himself. It stemmed from a built-in rhythm he is born with. This led to a stylised form of movement and, later still, to the classical way of performing.

Dancing's prestige was at its highest in ancient Greek times. One of the seven Muses was Terpsichore, the Muse who presided over dancing. Greek boys and girls danced naked before statues of the gods in religious rites.

The primitive dancer generally follows a set pattern. He dances barefoot, wears a mask or paints his face and body, and adorns himself with magic talismans. All these customs usually have some deep religious significance.

Even though the primitive has an extraordinary sense of rhythm, his skill and technique count for little compared with his ritual and powers of endurance. Repetition has a hypnotic effect, not only on himself, but also on his audiences.

In Asian countries some of the dances date back thousands of years, having been performed with little or no alteration all that time.

Only in recent years has Eastern dancing been seen, let alone appreciated, in the West, and it may be a long time before this highly civilised style is understood and valued here.

Some of the countries of South East Asia, which have India as a near-neighbour, like Thailand and Cambodia, owe their beautiful dances to the fact that the Indians once occupied their lands.

SPAIN

Every year Fiesta Gitana assembles a number of independent artistes who all specialise in Flamenco dancing. This is a mixture of Andalusian and Gypsy culture, which dates back to the mid-15th century, when gypsies first came to Spain.

Their dancing at that time was crude and uncivilised, and it did not reach perfection until the end of the last century. Since then, the Andalusian influence has lessened and the style of dancing is now almost entirely gypsy.

There are few true Flamenco artistes, so a new Fiesta Gitana is created every year to encourage the dancers. This enables them to gather together in a group and compete in friendly rivalry. In this way the standard is maintained —and a high standard it is!

Flamenco dancing demands the utmost dedication, and not everyone is prepared to face the hard work that it entails. The result of this has been that there is now a shortage of true Flamenco dancers and singers, and these now mainly specialise in only a few songs and dances, such as the Alegrias, Tanguillo, Soleares and Rhumba.

These dances are mostly performed with a 6–8 beat which is actually Latin American. They are danced quickly to give an impression of spontaneity.

The true Flamenco artiste is not always to be found on the professional stage, despite the large rewards that may be offered to him for taking part in this popular entertainment.

Above: *Dolores Amaya, younger sister of Spain's greatest gypsy dancer, Carmen Amaya, who had a fountain in the heart of Madrid and a theatre named after her. Dolores is here seen dancing a Bulerias with superb intensity and capturing the style that made her sister so famous.*

Left: *Curro Velez, one of the supreme exponents of this rare and inbred art, in a number of positions.* **Above:** *Two of the many fascinating features of true Spanish dancing are the swirling colours and the rhythmic stamping of the feet that fire the senses of the dancers and their audience. For all the abandon, the movements are absolutely classical.*

Some of the best dancing is, in fact, seen at local fiestas or private parties. Andalusians seem to perform most memorably when they are surrounded by the sort of atmosphere that only their fellow-countrymen can supply. They are temperamental people and very conscious of their surroundings. This is hardly surprising when we remember that Flamenco started as a tribal and nomadic art and that the only spectators were the members of wandering, colourful groups of gypsies.

Above and right: *A notable feature of Flamenco dancing is the Zapateado. It entails beating a fast tattoo with the heels, while the hands, which hold the inevitable castanets, keep time to the stamping.*

Above: *Two stars of the company, Carmen Casarrubios and Curro Velez, posed in that proud attitude adopted by every Flamenco dancer.*

HUNGARY

Left and above: *Members of the Hungarian State Dance Company wearing costumes which are not unlike the dresses they wear for festivals at home. The costumes are all highly embroidered with the utmost skill, and the colours are brilliant—as audiences expect them to be!*

During the 18th century the Hungarian czardas reigned supreme in the hearts of all true subjects of the Austro-Hungarian Empire. Even the czardas, however, could not stand up to the incredible popularity of the waltz, which first swept through central Europe at the end of the century and then became all the rage in Paris, London, New York and the rest of the civilised world.

Yet on the Hungarian plains the true plainsman never forsook the dance of his ancestors and despised the new craze for the waltz. As far as he was concerned it was no match for the virile czardas!

When the Hungarian State Dance Company visited Britain recently, people expected exciting and uninhibited displays of folk dancing—and got them!

One particularly spectacular number was the Bottle Dance, in which the dancers pirouetted at great speed with a full wine bottle balanced on their heads! This is a feat only equalled by some African Witch Doctors.

Above left: *The spectacular Bottle Dance.* **Below:** *A variation of the Hungarian czardas.*

Right: *The virile dancing of the Magyar Plainsmen, a unique display of enthusiasm and fire.*

JAPANESE RITUAL

Really to appreciate these colourful but simple dances to the full, they should be seen in their serene native setting. But, as many Westerners know, they are enjoyable anywhere.

The ritual of Japanese dancers begins with their make-up. This is lavishly applied and takes a long time to put on—some meticulous dancers take hours!

The hair is arranged in a style that has not changed for centuries. The foundation colour is the same dead white for every role, and onto it is sketched the expression and character of the role the dancer will be assuming.

Costumes are seldom changed, yet such is the complete artistry of these dancers that each performance varies in subtle shades of interpretation. This naturally makes repetitions all the more fascinating to observe.

Every movement has a special meaning. It may depict a young woman waiting for her lover, or an oafish country bumpkin, courting the lady he longs for so hopelessly. All the movements are very closely followed by the audience, who are just as critical as any group of ballet-lovers in the West.

Japanese dancing is an acquired taste—like oysters or olives! Yet it is well worth the acquiring. Once it is understood it becomes entertaining and fascinating.

Two famous Japanese dancers, Suzushi Hanayagi and Sususetsu Hanayagi, demonstrating some very stylised movements in the Kabuki and Jiuta dances. Note the ever-present fan.

Today, if we wish to write down the steps of any ballet, we have a system called "notation", which can be followed in any part of the world. The ancient Egyptians had no such system, but they chiselled out the various movements of their ritualistic dances on stone.

Now, after 5,000 years, these dances have been brought to life once more by the talented dancer from Tanzania, Parin Stoll.

THE
TEMPLE DANCERS
OF
ANCIENT EGYPT

To become a temple dancer in ancient Egypt was considered a great honour. Only young girls from the most select families were chosen. They were taken from their parents at the age of six and were sent to special schools for training by the priests of the temples in which they were later to perform.

In some of the more important of these ceremonies the Pharaohs and their Queens took part themselves, usually representing the god Amun and his divine wife, Mut.

The Egyptians believed that their dances and music were destined to be eternal, and, in fact, one of their dances, the Zar, is still performed in Egypt today, some 5,000 years later. Because the choreography of the dances was part of the Egyptians' religious ritual, it was preserved with the utmost care.

Every large temple had its chorus and its troupe of dancers, the largest being the vast Karnak Temple of Upper Nile, which had a huge hall called the House of Song. Here, in the 18th Dynasty, the glory of this ancient culture reached its zenith. In fact, there was a magnificent renaissance of all the arts at this time, very like the Renaissance period in Europe many centuries later.

Much of our knowledge of ancient Egypt's dance and music is due to the work of rediscovery carried out by the composer, Denis Gray Stoll, and his dancer wife

The BRITISH CLASSIC

CINDERELLA is called *Zolushka* in Russia and *Cendrillon* in France. It was first produced in England at the King's Theatre in London in 1822. The story was adapted from Perrault's version of the old story, and the ballet was later produced in many other countries, including Russia and France.

The Royal Ballet's *Cinderella* has Sir Frederick Ashton's choreography and Prokofiev's music. No other company so brilliantly captures the spirit of this fairytale ballet. It has become a British classic!

Opposite are two great ballerinas, the incomparable Margot Fonteyn and the superb South African technician, Nadia Nerina, who recently retired at the height of her career. Both are dressed in Cinderella's second act costume.

Below right is a court scene and in the centre is Fonteyn as Cinderella at midnight!

Grupo Gulbenkian de Bailado

FOR originality during 1969 the accolade should go to Walter Gore for his *Ensaio de Dance e Movimento*. The ballet was first performed in Lisbon in February, 1969, and danced to the music of three composers—Bach, Rabe and Hambraeus.

The ballet opens with the choreographer walking on to the stage and arranging the lighting! The artists stroll nonchalantly on and begin their loosening-up exercises. All this time the audience is wondering if the stage manager has forgotten to lower the curtain! As the class warms up and the dancers take their appointed places, the music begins, and we watch the choreographer creating his ballet. The class progresses, while he repeats, corrects, improvises and improves, conducting his dancers as though they were an orchestra.

Soon, the form of the ballet is moulded and understood by all: then, the audience can almost feel the exhilaration felt by the dancers.

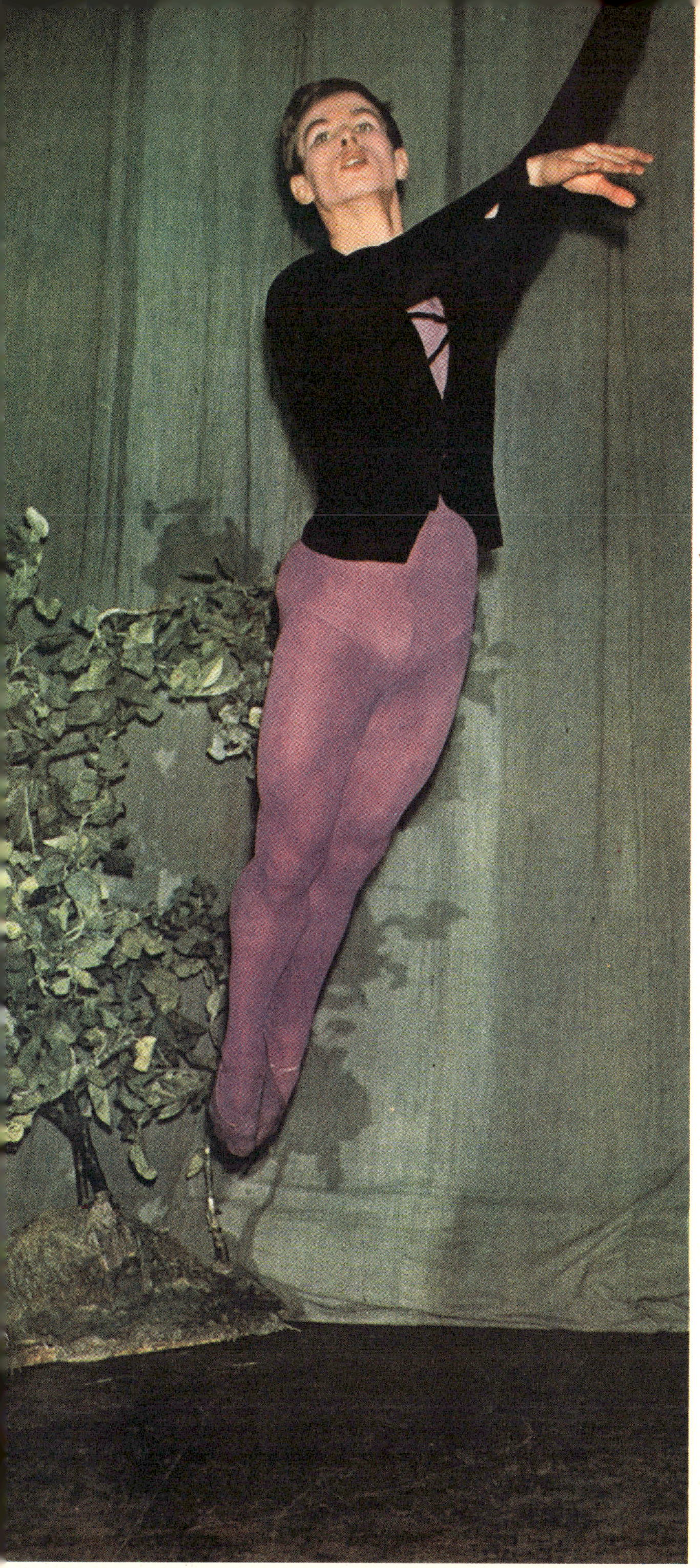

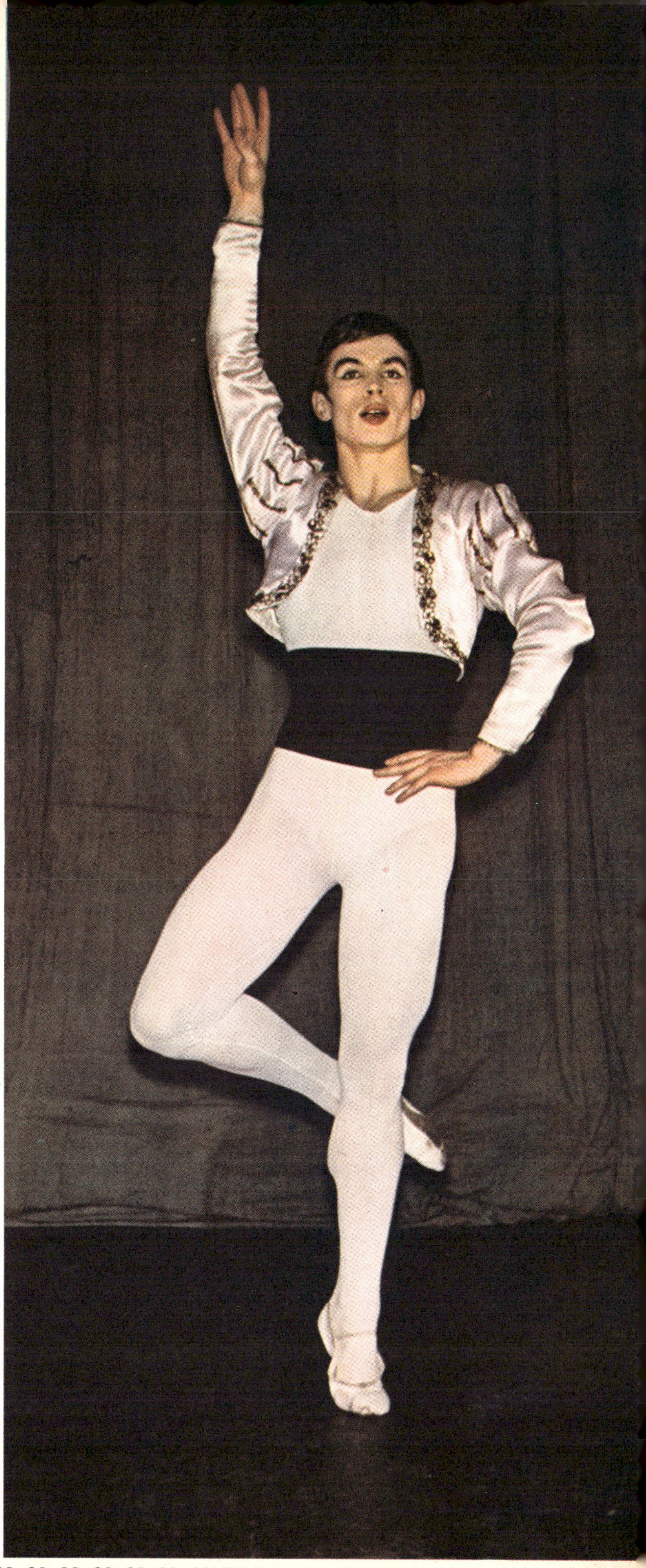

Magic Moments

Two rare colour photographs of Rudolf Nureyev taken in Russia before he defected to the West. On the left he is seen as Albrecht in Giselle, *and on the right in the ballet,* Don Quixote.

The Royal Ballet's Biggest Success

La Fille Mal Gardée is one of the oldest ballets in the Royal Ballet's current repertoire and it has proved its biggest post-war success. It is sometimes called The Wayward Daughter, or Vain Precautions.

Left: *Lise, danced by Nadia Nerina, and her sweetheart, Colas, the persistent suitor, danced by David Blair.*
Top right: *Another picture of the two young lovers.*
Right and far right: *A harvesting scene and a Grand Jeté by that superb technician, Nadia Nerina.*
Below right and far right: *Another harvesting scene, and a public declaration of love by Colas to his sweetheart. A live pony is used to draw the dog-cart, whose manners are not all that they should be! However, it always delights the audience.*

T HE STORY of this tremendously popular ballet is a simple one of true love finding a way. Needless to say, the course of true love does not run smoothly!

Lise, the daughter of a widow named Simone, is engaged, much against her will, to a rich neighbour's son called Alain. He is not very bright and Lise finds it impossible to take him seriously.

As the plot progresses, Lise and Colas find that the persistent chaperoning of her is a challenge which has to be overcome—with disastrous results. However, all is well in the end. Colas and Lise are forgiven, much to the joy of all the villagers, and, amid great rejoicing, the lovers are married and live happily ever after.

The Royal Ballet's version of La Fille mal Gardée was created for Nadia Nerina.

A DANCER'S WORLD

Above left: *Australian-born ballerina, Marilyn Burr, waiting in the wings for her entrance during a dress rehearsal of* Don Quixote, *and wearing leg warmers to keep her muscles supple.*

Above right: *When Jane Landon was a Royal Ballet School student, she danced Aurora in the annual school performance. She is shown here in the star dressing room with Fonteyn's own dresser.*

Left: *Three great stars of the ballet world—from left to right, Anton Dolin, Rudolf Nureyev and Janine Charrat seen discussing some technical points during a rehearsal.*

Right: *After a performance a conductor goes backstage to wait for his curtain call, which he takes with the artists. Here is Festival Ballet's Aubrey Bowman, waiting for his call.*

Right: *Some of the girls of the Theatre class of the Arts Educational School relaxing after a performance. They have forgotten the tension they felt before the show.*

Below right: *Going off-stage to her dressing room after a performance at the Festival Hall, Belinda Wright stops to chat for a few moments with a colleague.*

Above: *Lesley Odell studies the design of a new costume for her.*
Left: *Lesley and Jan Cave are pictured with the Costume Centre's designer, who is preparing designs for them.*

Choosing a Costume

EVERYONE loves dressing up, and one of the most exciting things in the world of ballet is the make-believe of assuming a strange character and then dressing up for the part!

Two young dancers, Jan Cave of the Arts Educational School and Lesley Odell, ex-Royal Ballet School, both of them 18 years old, recently had the exciting opportunity of choosing their own dresses at the new London Costume Centre. Needless to say, they had a marvellous time.

The only trouble was that there were so many dresses for them to try on, so many hats to admire themselves in and so many things to be seen at the Centre that by the end of their visit they were quite exhausted. Not that they complained about that!

James Parker and his co-director, Valerie Hyman, were most helpful to the two girls and insisted on giving them a personally conducted tour of the huge wardrobe salons. It was certainly a visit to remember!

Above: *Lesley and Jan are pictured discussing the designs during a fitting, as they wait for the dressmaker.*

Left: *The actual designs that the two girls are looking at, which look just right for a new dancing project.*

Above: *James Parker and Valerie show the girls some of the colourful materials used in making up the dresses.* **Below:** *Jan studies the intricate work that goes into making a garment.*

Above: *One of the craftswomen making some hand lace for a particular costume.* **Below:** *The two girls visit the cutting-room where much of the work takes place.*

Magic Moments

A touching moment at the end of the second act of Swan Lake, *in which Karl Musil as Prince Siegfried pleads with Galina Samtsova as Odette to leave the evil Rothbart (Jean Pierre Alban).*

BALLET WITH A NEW

IN 1957, at a time when British audiences were being offered little but the standard classics, a group of dancers formed themselves into a company called the Western Theatre Ballet. Their aim was to pioneer short, livelier ballets about subjects the larger companies ignored.

They made their headquarters in the West of England at Bristol, and, contrary to all expectations, they were immediately successful—so much so that they set a pattern which has almost become a blueprint for small companies today.

Like all pioneers, they had a hard time making ends meet. Members of the Company did all the chores usually done by hired helps. The music was improvised for each ballet, then taped. Their hardships proved a blessing, as the type of performances they evolved proved highly suitable for television. When they appeared in London, the critics praised them highly. Their headquarters is now in Glasgow, so they are now the Scottish Theatre Ballet!

LOOK

Scenes from some of the ballets performed on television by this talented young group. On the opposite page and right are two shots from an amusing piece called Little Nothings. Below is a scene from Non Stop, a jazz dance in which the girl exhausts all her partners, and at the bottom of the page are two scenes from a hilarious skit called Street Games.

The Company was originally founded by the late Elizabeth West and Peter Darrell.

The Sleeping

TCHAIKOVSKY's score for *The Sleeping Beauty* is quite the most brilliant ballet music he ever wrote. The first performance of this world famous and greatly loved ballet took place in 1890 at the Maryinsky Theatre, St. Petersburg (now Leningrad).

The Tsar of Russia had attended the dress rehearsal. He was unimpressed by Tchaikovsky's music, and all he said to the unfortunate composer was: "Very nice!" The critics also were cool, but the public loved it.

The choreographer of *The Sleeping Beauty* was Petipa. Working closely with the composer, he poured all his genius into the creation of some of the most famous variations in all ballet, including the Blue Bird pas de deux, the Rose Adagio, the Vision scene, and the adagio for Aurora (the Sleeping Beauty) and her Prince.

It is hardly surprising that Leningrad's *Sleeping Beauty*

Above: *Irina Kolpakova being held high in a superb lift by her partner, Vladilen Semyonov, during their adagio.* **Left:** *The finale.*

Above: *The seductive cat in one of the amusing variations during the last act of the ballet.*

Above: *Another scene from the finale, which shows the numerical strength of the Kirov Ballet and the lavishness of its presentation.*

Beauty

has maintained the highest standards down the years. Perhaps no company in the world has the same classical grace and lyrical qualities as the Kirov's—the Maryinsky Theatre became the Kirov in 1935. The performance of its ballerina, Irina Kolpakova, as Aurora is as near perfection as is possible for a dancer. It seems incredible that anyone so slender and fragile-looking can perform such amazing feats of agility and strength with such supreme elegance and apparent ease.

Although Kolpakova is principal ballerina of the Kirov, she is also in great demand as a guest artist at the Bolshoi Theatre in Moscow. As for *The Sleeping Beauty*, it has remained for over eighty years one of the most popular of all ballets, and has been performed all over the world.

Top right: *The Blue Bird pas de deux is a most difficult variation to dance.* **Top left:** *Another of the numerous variations.* **Centre right:** *The beautiful pas de deux of Aurora and her Prince.* **Centre left:** *The Lilac Fairy, a role second only to that of Aurora's.*

Above: *Irina Kolpakova in scenes from the second act after the Prince has awakened her with a kiss.*

Above: *The whole Court joins in the celebrations for Aurora's awakening and her marriage to the Prince.*

A class with Ivor Meggido is like being in a boxing ring, but all the dancers enjoy it. Keith Beckett is in the striped-blue sweater.

A MODERN CLASS

THE discipline and sheer hard work of the dance world are truly democratic. No distinctions or concessions are made to rank, and only the dedicated can hope to survive—let alone keep ahead—in a very competitive profession.

All dancers have to do their daily barre if they are to keep fit, whatever their position in a company—the newest recruit or the star ballerina.

This page includes pictures of Keith Beckett, a brilliant producer and director of musical extravaganzas. He was at one time a principal male dancer with the Festival Ballet. He is seen here taking part in a mixed class given by Ivor Meggido. With Keith, as with the youngest coryphée, it is a labour of love.

ALICIA MARKOVA

ALICIA MARKOVA ranks as the first great English ballerina. She set a standard by which all later English dancers have been judged. From 1963 until 1969 she directed the Metropolitan Opera Ballet in New York.

Critics have described Markova as the reincarnation of the fabulous Marie Taglioni, the Swedish-born dancer who made pointe dancing popular, created the ballerina-length dress, and parted her hair in the middle. Taglioni was particularly acclaimed for her weightlessness—she seemed to float in the air—a quality so suitable for the Romantic ballets.

The picture shows Markova as Taglioni in her Pas de Quatre costume.

Above: *Young boys and girls start their lessons in
the Rambert tradition at an early age.*
Right: *One of the most poignant moments in Giselle
in which the heroine stabs herself after finding
that she has been betrayed.*

The RAMBERT TRADITION

DAME MARIE RAMBERT was born in Warsaw in 1888. She was influenced, like so many others in the early years of the century, by the great American dance reformer, Isadora Duncan.

In 1906, Myriam Ramberg (as she then was) came to Paris to study medicine and give dance recitals. Four years later, she joined Jacques Dalcroze's school in Geneva and went with him to St. Petersburg to demonstrate his methods.

She was chosen by Diaghilev and Nijinsky to help them with the new ballet, *Le Sacre du Printemps,* which opened sensationally in Paris in 1913. It was the start of a great career which has meant so much to the many dancers, choreographers and artists she has trained and encouraged down the years.

It was Marie Rambert's Ballet Club, founded in 1930 in her husband's Mercury Theatre in London, that helped give British ballet such a wonderful start. Her Ballet Rambert is Britain's oldest company.

Although the Ballet Rambert has never been very strong in numbers, it has made up for this by its classical excellence. Some of its productions of Giselle *(left) have never been bettered.*

Danseur Noble

ALTHOUGH Vincent Warren has a faultless classical style as well as a strong, romantic bearing, he is equally at home in modern and contemporary dancing. He bears a strong physical resemblance to Rudolf Nureyev.

Les Grands Ballets Canadiens visited Europe last year and this young dancer was singled out for special praise.

Vincent Warren possesses a pure Russian classical technique, together with extraordinary elevation, yet, surprisingly enough, he is Canadian-trained.

Recently, he has been greatly helped by one of the finest male dancers of all time, our own world-famous Anton Dolin, who is artistic advisor to the Company.

Balletomanes should eagerly watch out for future appearances by this fabulous young dancer.

Young choreographers in the making

THE Nesta Brooking School in London's Marylebone High Street is a very exceptional ballet school. Its students do not simply learn to dance: they also learn to create ballets.

Nesta Brooking, who is herself a choreographer, has found that a number of young dancers are potential choreographers and she has developed ways of training them to take the most of their talents. The best of the ballets created by her students are good enough to be performed by professional companies, and all of them have some interest, showing a sense of form, and effectively putting across a theme or an idea.

The students who dance in these newly-created ballets find the experience they have gained invaluable when they join ballet companies. There, they find themselves being rehearsed by choreographers who expect them to perform patterns of movement in an exciting and meaningful way, and, because of their experience in Nesta Brooking's school, they can respond flexibly and imaginatively to the demands made on them. They have learned that dancing is more than doing steps correctly.

As for the students who have been learning choreography in the school, they have had the experience needed to become the professional choreographers of tomorrow. They have not only learned how to put dance movements together, but also about the other arts which are so essential to a choreographer—music, painting, sculpture and drama.

In the early stages, working on very simple composition exercises, each student is likely to find difficulty in some aspect of choreography. It may be in coming to grips with the music, or spacing out the dance across the room, or finding the right steps to go with an idea. In later composition

At the Nesta Brooking School all students are encouraged to design their own ballets

classes, Nesta Brooking gives exercises designed to help cope with these special difficulties, and so they gradually learn how to tackle more and more complicated exercises, using a number of dancers instead of just one. For example, she might ask them to observe very carefully what happens at a party and then recreate this as choreography, first as a mime scene, and then using dance movements to make it into a small ballet.

After a year or so, students are ready to create short ballets of their own. They choose a suitable piece of music, classical or modern, or, perhaps, get some specially composed. They then select dancers from among the other students and rehearse them. Nesta Brooking helps them shape their ideas— pointing out, for example, that the "picture" of one piece of grouping is ill-balanced, with too many dancers on one side—but the final result is very much their own.

Magic Moments

Jean Babilée and Gerda Daum, principal dancers of the Hamburg Opera Ballet, gazing at the awe-inspiring ruins at Baalbek in the Lebanon where they performed in "L'Histoire du Soldat."

THE
PIONEER

BORN in America at the end of the last century, Martha Graham has been a remarkable pioneer of modern and contemporary dance. So great is her influence, that nearly all schools of modern ballet owe the basic structure of their movements to this wonderful woman.

Choreographer of over a hundred ballets, and principal teacher in her own world-famous school, Martha Graham still finds the time and energy to star with her company on most of its world tours. Her name on the bills means a packed audience. She is certainly one of the greatest dancers of all time.

*Scenes from the ballet **Phaedra**, a Greek tragedy written over 2,000 years ago. So great is the dramatic personality and power of Martha Graham that she vividly brings this ancient legend to life.*

VIENNA

Dancers of the

THE Vienna Opera House is one of the most beautiful and best-equipped theatres in the world. It is the pride and joy of every Viennese. Until recently, dancing has come a poor second to singing in the hearts of the opera-loving Austrians, but since the arrival of the new ballet-master, Wazlaw Orlikowsky, things have changed. This brilliant, Kirov-trained choreographer has transformed ballet in Vienna.

Orlikowsky has revitalised the Company, sending his dancers off on world-wide tours and also creating for them some of the most spectacular ballets ever seen in central Europe. The standard of dancing has so improved that Vienna's is now one of Europe's finest classical ballet companies.

The Opera House has to be seen to be believed. Its stage occupies at least half of its total area: it is larger than the auditorium! Backstage, everything appears vast and complicated. When scenery has to be loaded, 30 ton diesel trucks drive right on to the stage to do it!

Above: *Erika Zlocha.* **Below left:** *Paul Vondrak and Lisl Maar.*
Below right: *The Corps de Ballet in the costume of* **Etude**
rehearses in one of the magnificent reception halls of the
Opera House. **Right:** *A posed group from* **Les Sylphides**—
Lilly Scheuermann, Michael Birkmeyer, Gisela Cech, and in
the foreground, Susie Kirnbauer.

STATE OPERA BALLET

city of music and song in their fabulous Opera House

Scenes from the variations on the famous Viennese waltz, which this company perform so charmingly and with the gaiety one expects from the true Viennese.

THE VOLKSOPER

THE WALTZ as we know it today is a refined version of an old German peasant dance called the Landler. The actual word "waltz" comes from the Latin for "to turn".

Musicians carried its gay rhythms and its tunes down the Danube, and as it reached the cities in the 18th century, it became more civilised. The custom of throwing girls high in the air was dropped, and so were the hob-nail boots the peasants wore for the dance!

Waltz fever swept Europe in the early 19th century. Great composers like Schubert and Chopin wrote waltzes, while in mid-century Vienna the Strauss family composed Viennese waltzes which have enchanted millions for over a century.

The small but delightful Theater an der Wien, known as the Volksoper, is the home of the Volksoper Ballet. In this historic theatre, where famous operettas, ballets and operas had their premières, the strains of some of the most popular waltzes ever written were first heard.

More variations on the same theme. The long flowing dresses make a striking contrast to the abbreviated skirt, or, rather, tutu on the left. But whatever the costume the music is a waltz—by Strauss, Lehar or another waltz-king.

BALLET OF VIENNA

The three pictures shown here demonstrate the remarkable variety and range of dancing the Company includes in its programmes. **Left:** *The peasants' flag-waving dance.* **Right:** *A typical modern moment.* **Above:** *A classical jump.*

This young and appealing troupe of artists is not technically as perfect as some of the great international companies, but what the dancers lack in skill they make up for in variety and charm. For sheer entertainment value they are often more worthwhile to watch than some more accomplished companies. Too often the real reason for ballet is forgotten in trying for technical perfection.

Left: *Some of the girls in colourful peasant costumes relaxing on the stage during the playing of the overture, as they wait for the stage manager's warning call of "Curtain going up!"*

Magic Moments

Irina Borowska and Oleg Briansky in the wonderful pas de deux in the first act of Swan Lake, *where Prince Siegfried pledges his undying love for Odette, the Swan Queen.*

THE ABSTRACT WORLD OF *Alwin Nikolais*

U NDERSTANDING abstract art in the form of paintings is difficult for many people. Yet if the picture ceases to be static, if the figures and objects move rhythmically, then it soon becomes an art which almost everyone can understand.

This fact has long been realised by Alwin Nikolais, a man of futuristic imagination, who has been called the Picasso of modern ballet. It probably accounts for the fantastic success of his company whenever and wherever it appears.

It was in the spring of 1956 that Alwin Nikolais, with a company of seven dancers, exploded on to the dance scene with a new ballet called *Kaleidoscope* at the American Dance Festival of Connecticut College. The audience's enthusiasm knew no bounds. So great was the ovation given him that it was instantly recognised that a brilliant new choreographer had come to stay. His startlingly beautiful work was clearly the blueprint of a trend to follow—for those who had the ability to!

Unfortunately, Nikolais' work

sets almost too high a standard of perfection, and his ballets are still ten years ahead of their time.

Nikolais paints a picture with living figures against a background of vivid, flaming colour, accompanied by music on stereophonic tape that is equally way-out and bizarre.

These psychedelic and dazzling performances have a mesmeric effect on the audiences who watch them. They range far beyond the usual theatrical limits. His effects are astounding.

Nikolais has long been admired for his superb television productions. Now, with the wider use of colour on the small screen, his ability to use this medium to the full is expected to result in a series of television masterpieces.

For a number of years now this great and unusual creative artist has evolved an entirely new concept of ballet, some would say of theatre itself. The tantalising question remains, however—is he going too fast for anyone to be able to follow in his footsteps? All ballet lovers should enjoy finding out the answer!

Masks, Props and Mobiles all help give these way-out ballets their unique "look". But even more important a feature of Alwin Nikolais' strange and exciting work is his use of lighting and colour.

Imago, *one of the Company's weirder creations. Elongated, falsely-jointed limbs startle the eye.*

900376-99-6